PROTECTING
THE MENTALLY
CHALLENGED
YOUNG ADULT

PROTECTING THE MENTALLY CHALLENGED YOUNG ADULT

SHELLEY ROSE

Copyright © 2013 by Shelley Rose.

Library of Congress Control Number:		2013900923
ISBN:	Hardcover	978-1-4797-8045-7
	Softcover	978-1-4797-8044-0
	eBook	978-1-4797-8046-4

This book is based from a true story.

This book was printed in the United States of America.

Rev. Date: 01/03/2014

To order additional copies of this book, contact:
Xlibris LLC
1-888-795-4274
www.Xlibris.com
Orders@Xlibris.com
126916

The silence and the emptiness of the joys, smiles and just a simple conversation is really so much to bear when there are so many thoughts and decisions to be made and no one to discuss this with especially those that you can trust.

In Memory of My Mother Sadie Golub. To my daughter and her grandmother (who never got to hug her again) and to all those that are like her. She is the love of my life, and I think of her with every breath I take.

INTRODUCTION

The law states that when a person turns eighteen, they are considered an adult, and the definition means physically mature and not mentally. They don't tell you that if you are mentally challenged, the government is giving you financial and medical help. When this person is over eighteen, they will not protect this person if they are abducted, coerced, mind-manipulated, exploited, and alienated from those who raised them unless you get guardianship, because this person is now considered an adult. It is not stressed that when this person becomes eighteen, you need to become a guardian to protect that child, and in order to do so, you will need your own attorney, who will cost no less than $2,000 or more even though you have given up your life for those more than eighteen years that he or she was with you. Another thing the government doesn't tell you is that there are no *agencies* that can help young adults over eighteen who could be stolen or abducted or coerced or brainwashed or that can help you protect your child.

The AMBER Alert Law is another problem as it does not include people that are mentally challenged after age eighteen. They also don't tell you that this young adult can go to any Social Security Office with a stranger, and so long as that child says yes and they are over sixteen, the payee, which you were, can be changed into that stranger's name. This change could even be the name of your ex-spouse, who never even paid child support and had all the checks sent to them. It doesn't matter who you are; you can be an ex-con, a bum on the street, or anyone over eighteen as they don't check out who the person is so long as the handicapped person who is over sixteen gives their permission even if they read and write like a third or a fourth grader and whose IQ is 57.

It's very, very upsetting that people who have given up their lives for sixteen years or more can't get help for their child/adult without having to go for guardianship and spending monies they may not have when they should become an "automatic guardian" or at least the person who has custody and has cared for this person who has been in special education classes. The thoughts are, if this person dies, then let the next person have to pay for guardian. The AMBER Law is something else that needs to be changed by adding that anyone who is mentally challenged should be included, whereas the AMBER Law only protects those up to age eighteen.

People/families that know the laws will know that a person over eighteen and without a guardianship can be stolen, swayed, brainwashed, or coerced and could be put into a cultic situation where someone who is so vulnerable doesn't have a clue what is happening to them. There are families that will cut all the individual's connections to his/her family (which is a cultic situation), brainwash them by telling this person that their families do not want them or love them, and just sway this weak-minded person to where they believe what they are told. They could be threatened to instill fear as people did with Elizabeth Smart (a normal fourteen-year-old who was abducted). If they cut out all their rights to speak to their families and friends, then they will have no one to tell them what is right or to get other opinions from as they are not allowed to listen to anyone but those that have stolen them as they become the new authority figure in their life, telling them what to do and how to do it and when to do it and who has learned to push their buttons.

That's right, a "normal" family or just one person that you may know or think you know can take your young adult and coerce them to go wherever they want to, and because you didn't get guardianship, there is nothing anyone can do because they are over eighteen years of age and considered an adult. If you try to get guardianship, you have to hope and pray that the judge will listen to the people going after the ward. The guardianship law stating that "the 'ward' has the right to decide where they want to live" needs to be revised as well. The three panelists who need to propose their reports to the courts should all have professional experience with mentally challenged people rather than not have any experience as they aren't qualified as an Educator teaching or understanding special education. A specialist in this field is now required in all schools as it was discovered in the late sixties and early seventies how important this is to those that need special care. In the past years, this was not the case. The law for a panelist who needs to see this person states that he is not required to be a specialist in this field of special needs.

The other problem is that the panelist should not be allowed to speak to anyone other than the mentally challenged person and should speak to the two attorneys involved to know how to deal with whatever the problem is so that they can make a more accurate report on behalf of the mentally challenged person, but this is not the case. They should be told to take this person out of their environment and away from those that may be an influence to that person rather than to stay in another room of their house. The reason for this is that if a person has been mind-manipulated or swayed, being out of the environment that they are in may put this person more at ease, and they will feel more comfortable in speaking to this panelist. The adult child may feel that being in a different environment where no one could hear them will make them speak more openly and freely, as they should.

The three panelists picked to see if this person is competent should be aware of any problems so they can derive with a more accurate report by speaking to everyone. The panelists should not be allowed to make comments about the custodian, as one of the panelists who was not "specialized" wrote to the courts that the "mother was detrimental" without speaking or seeing this person. How can they make comments without knowing all sides?

A bud is just the beginning of a new Chapter in life as we are all
"Authors to Our Own Life".

A sun sets, but it will always come up and this is what you always look forward to as you will need to take a long deep breath to get your strength and regain your thoughts to continue, as the sun will rise again you will too and be ready for the next chapter.

CHAPTER I

❖

There was a family called the Clowns, who stole a very normal-looking young lady who was mentally challenged and could not make decisions. The Clowns, who wanted a girl and wanted her money to keep their son happy by using her as a sex toy, stole this young lady named Becky, who is thirty-three years old, has almost-black hair, green eyes, and is a little overweight and so bubbly and affectionate and cute as a button. She was kept from her family for four years until her mother finally found an attorney to help her proceed and try to get her daughter back. The reason it took so long is because it was a very small town in the middle of no place.

She couldn't get an attorney to do the work because it became such an unusual guardianship, and they just couldn't be bothered, so she thought. She had the police, who could do nothing because Becky was already brainwashed into telling them she didn't want to see or speak to her mother, when in fact, at the beginning and when Becky had the opportunity, she would call her mother until they took out the phones and told her she had better not call her mother again. Her mother had hired a private investigator and called the abuse center, which sent out investigators who could only see if she was dressed and fed according to the government rules. All she was doing was spinning her wheels because Becky was over eighteen and considered an adult, and there was no guardian.

Becky never knew what the consequences would be by saying she didn't want to see or speak to her mother. She did not want to speak to her mother because the Clowns told her that her mother didn't love her and didn't want her anymore, and they would remind her each time something came up. Becky was told to say she was very happy there, so when the police would do a "well-being" check where she was living, they couldn't do a thing because Becky was considered an adult, and so their hands were tied. Sheila sent the police over to Becky's at least three times, with hopes that she would see and speak to her, but they couldn't go again as they told Sheila (Becky's mom) that they were fearful of being sued for harassment. They really became very cautious and couldn't help even though they thought Sheila was right. Sheila was 5'2", slim, with dark-brown eyes and a beautiful smile that devoted her life to both of her children. Sheila was a special education teacher and was Becky's custodian and parent for thirty years.

One of the officers even told Sheila he would try to steal Becky if this was his daughter, but even that was impossible because they watched her 24-7 and couldn't get near her. Sheila was afraid to be near the house as they could sue her for harassment or trespassing and would try to get a restraining order out against her. There was no place to hide or be hidden from this house as it was a community of homes that were next to one another with no cars on the streets and no place to walk. Sheila did think of doing this, but she also knew it was not legal although it went through her mind.

By not having guardianship, the problems just escalated and made it more difficult for Sheila to just go to an attorney who would file the proper papers for guardianship and be done with it. It's not easy going into a small town in the middle of no place to find the right attorney, especially when there are only five or six at the most who specialize in guardianships and who would be willing to help fight against someone who says, "I am happy and do not want to speak to my mother," because in a guardianship, the ward, who is Becky, can make the decision to live where she wants. If the courts awarded full guardianship, then Becky would not have these rights. Finding an attorney that has dealt with cases like this is few and far between and very expensive, so you need to find one that will just believe the mother when she says that her daughter was put into a cultic situation and that this person has been brainwashed. In time, the mother has to find the proper professional help in order to make Becky understand how much her family loves her and how wrong these people were and how they lied to her. The mother should not give up the fight if she really does love her child and knows that the things this child is saying are because she has been told by these strangers to say them. There are no agencies for young adults that have been stolen or abducted that would help protect them and you. There is an abuse agency that will send an investigator out to see if the young adult is eating and being clothed, but that is all they can do and, of course, if she was being abused physically. The catch to this is, it would have to be physical abuse and not mental. They don't know your child and have no way of comparing this child as a "before and after" because they don't speak to the person who raised this young adult. If an investigator goes out, the report could read, "She is happy and does not want to see her mother" and is being fed and clothed and is not being abused as far as he/she can see, which means that once again, there is nothing that could be done.

How can a stranger know your child when you are the only one who raised your child? How can strangers such as the police or investigator detect that this child has been brainwashed and told what to say? Becky was not taken out of the environment but spoken to in the house with the Clowns in the next room.

A parent who has pictures and reports and letters and who was a special education teacher and has had her daughter in her care for thirty years should be creditable enough (so you would think), and according to the guardianship laws, it's up to the way an attorney presents his case. In Sheila's case, her attorney said nothing. If an attorney doesn't want to try, then you must not give up, and you must go to the next attorney until you find one that will try and then pray he will be good.

Unfortunately, Sheila couldn't change attorneys because right from the beginning, the attorney she ended up with was terrible and made so many mistakes that when she tried to get another attorney, a new attorney would not take the case from where he left off. Another problem you can run across is everyone perceives something the way they want to, and even though you aren't supposed to judge a person until all the evidence is in, they do.

A judge runs his courtroom as he sees fit, even though it may not be right. They tell you that you can appeal a case, but they don't tell you that you will need at least $15,000 or more to get this done.

A judge should listen to those who are fighting for guardianship if there is more than one person and not just look at what three panelists (who aren't necessarily experienced with the mentally challenged) or others have to say. It's very sad that these three panelists have this much authority to make up a judge's mind when none of them know this mentally challenged person, especially in a forty-five-minute session. Some judges don't want to take the time to hear the whole story and would rather have every guardianship be the same. The court-appointed attorney (who can't wait until it's over), in this case, would not even take the time to speak to the biological mother as he only spoke to whom Becky was living with and Becky, who just shook her head to the questions he asked, like "I understand you wanted to live with the Clowns and not your mother." This court-appointed attorney would not take the time to hear all the facts. He only listens to the young adult, who reads and writes according to a third and fourth grader and whose IQ is a 57, and the people who kept her captive, instead of taking the time to speak to the person who raised this young adult. The attitude of the attorney was that he needed to grant this young adult her wishes, when he should have thought an investigation should have been done.

Nothing stays the same as there are always changes.

CHAPTER II

❖

Becky, who is now thirty-three years old, reads and writes like a third or fourth grader does and has an IQ of 57, has been in special education classes since she started school, and is considered an "educable mentally retarded." If it weren't for her mother, Becky would have been put into a "Down's syndrome" classroom, but Sheila found a school psychologist who would give Becky five exams until she found the right test to meet the criteria of Florida's standards to be in a "learning disabled" classroom versus a "Down's syndrome" classroom since Becky is normal looking.

Becky has this demeanor of going crazy over young men. She was stolen/coerced and brainwashed by this family more than once, but this time, they finally succeeded. Becky wasn't the only girl they tried to steal as there were two others, but they didn't succeed. They convinced Becky that her family was bad and that they didn't love her, which made her very angry that she didn't want to go home, not realizing she could, but the Clowns wouldn't let her. Sheila (Becky's mom), after three and a half years, finally found an attorney who would help her try to get her daughter back by going for the guardianship, but he was terrible and never represented Sheila in the three hearings they had in the courtroom as he told Sheila he would.

Sheila told the attorney that Becky was brainwashed, coerced, exploited, mind-manipulated, and was the victim of undue influence and proved each item to him. Sheila had letters from Lynn telling her how she was planning everything and how Becky was now going to call Lynn "Mom" and that Sheila would be considered her "ex-mom." Sheila showed him the documents and letters that they had Becky sign. They even had Becky sign the adoption papers when at this time, Becky was not married. They never had legal counsel for Becky, nor did they tell Sheila or her ex-husband. Lynn Clown wrote letters to Sheila, telling her that she would not be allowed to call Becky (they took out the phones in the house), and was told that she is not to write to Becky and that all mail would be sent back (Sheila did send a package, and it was sent back) and that she could not see Becky (as stated in Lynn's letters). Since the Clowns told Becky that her mother couldn't do anything, it only gave the Clowns more strength and showed Becky once again they were right. After a while, Becky believed whatever they said, especially when the police or the investigators couldn't do anything. But of course, Becky didn't understand or have any clues.

Everyone told Sheila to keep Becky from Robert (one of Lynn's sons), who has dirty brown hair, blue eyes, is soft in his middle, and thirty-one years old. Robert smokes, was on crack and cocaine, and is also manic-depressive, bipolar, a thief, abusive, and very vicious and lives in Crooksville, Florida. Becky, whose home used to be in New York but who has lived most of her life in Fort Lauderdale, Florida, was coerced into going to Crooksville, Florida, on January 15, 2001, by Robert and his mother. Becky once said that she didn't like Robert or his father, Larry, who is 5'10", fifty-seven years old, and is learning disabled, vicious, and not too bright. Lynn, who is a very strong person, is fifty-five years old, with gray hair, stands 5'4" and weighs three hundred pounds, wears glasses, and wears the pants in the family and knows just what buttons to push on Becky. Becky met Robert, who is two years younger than Becky, through Robert's brother, who is borderline retarded and who is the same age as Becky is. Lynn married this son to a girl who is also mentally challenged and is Hispanic, and she also tried to get her to stay in Brooksville with them but didn't succeed. Becky met them at a continued educational school that is an after-high school program for mentally challenged adults. Becky was invited over to their apartment one day, and that is how she met Robert.

Becky had a girlfriend whose name is Carol, who lived in Fort Lauderdale, Florida, with her parents. Carol is also learning disabled, whom Becky went to school with and was best friends with for years, but Carol has a higher IQ than Becky does. Carol and her parents asked Becky's mother, Sheila, if Becky could fly to visit with Carol for Carol's birthday for a week. They would do this with each other on numerous occasions throughout the years where Carol would visit Becky and then Becky would visit Carol. Sheila said "it would be okay," and so she gave Becky a round-trip ticket to fly to Fort Lauderdale, $250.00 for spending money, and a new cell phone to spend a week with her best friend in Fort Lauderdale, Florida. This was one of Becky's Christmas gifts. Before Becky left in November 2000, Sheila took Becky for her physical examination at the gynecologist's office to make sure everything was okay since she had sex with Robert in August. But what she didn't know is that Robert did not use protection as Lynn told him not to, and he got Becky pregnant. He stayed at Sheila's home for a short period until Sheila found he had stolen from her CDs, jewelry, VCR tapes, and was on drugs, so she told him to leave (in a nice way because she was afraid he would be destructive).

He moved his things out but still left a couple of things and told Sheila he would be back for the rest of his things. Sheila felt it was over, and being soft as she was, she let him stay overnight when he went back to get the rest of his things in her downstairs bedroom while Becky stayed upstairs. She didn't know the biggest fear she had was the fact that Becky would go downstairs where he was staying and had sex with him. This was the last time he went back to Sheila's. Becky and Robert did say that they had used protection whenever they had sex, especially since Becky couldn't take birth control pills as she was taking medication for seizures and was told she shouldn't take birth control pills. Nevertheless, Sheila thought she would rather be safe than sorry and had Becky at the gynecologist's office, where they told her she was okay, and they never knew she was pregnant. Becky never told Sheila that she contacted Robert before she left to visit her friend Carol in Fort Lauderdale as a boy-crazy teen whose memory is short and her friend Carol whom she hadn't seen in five months in Ft. Lauderdale, Florida. Becky flew to Fort Lauderdale on Saturday, January 15, 2002, to meet with her best friend, Carol, and her mother and, to Becky's surprise, her brother, who met Becky at the airport. Becky called Sheila (her mom) from the airport with her new cell phone to let Sheila know she arrived safely and to say hello to her brother.

Becky didn't tell anyone, but she had her friend Carol drive her to meet with Robert the next day, Sunday, January 16, 2002, at Sheila's other house that she still owned. Robert drove from Crooksville with his mother's permission to meet with Becky in Fort Lauderdale; so the only ones who knew they were going to meet were Robert and his mother. Sunday, at 12:00 a.m., Becky called her mother to tell her she was at the house that Sheila still owned and said, "Guess whom I met there, Robert."

She told Sheila that she thought Robert changed and that he was taking her out for dinner. When Becky left for Florida, she was very happy and called her mother to let her know she was all right. Robert planned to wine and dine her and take her to Disney World as mentally challenged people can be swayed very easily, and so Becky was like a kid with candy whose hormones were going one hundred miles an hour. Sheila immediately called Carol's mother and told her to get Becky away from Robert. Carol and her mother went over to get Becky and by the time they got there, Robert had already brainwashed Becky into not leaving by telling her how he was going to take her out for dinner. Sheila immediately called Robert and told him to put Becky back on the plane and even called Lynn, Robert's mother, to tell her the same thing. Lynn knew that Robert was going to take Becky up to Crooksville and tried to make it seem as though she had no idea whether he would put her back on the plane in Fort Lauderdale or take her to Crooksville. Lynn said, "If they come to Crooksville, should I put her on the plane when they arrive?" Sheila knew then she was on her way to Crooksville and told her to immediately put her on the plane. Sheila told

Lynn, "Becky's grandmother had a severe heart attack and doesn't have much longer to live. Please send her home." And then she proceeded to tell her, "She thought Becky was pregnant." Sheila lied to Lynn about Becky being pregnant as she took her to the doctor in November, and they never said anything about Becky being pregnant.

Lynn's other son, named Dick, is also learning disabled (she had two sons who were sick). They didn't want Robert or Dick, and so they proceeded to get Dick married to a Hispanic girl named Maria, who lived with her parents in Pompano Beach, Florida. At first, they thought Lynn and Larry would have Dick and Maria living near them and keep Maria and her check, which she received at the time from Social Security, until Becky came along, and both Lynn and Larry (Lynn's husband) liked Becky a lot more. Maria's family would call Maria and would tell her in Spanish to go home, so Lynn had no control. Lynn wanted their son Robert to be happy and stay out of Lynn's hair by getting Becky for him. In the meantime, Lynn called Social Security and told them Maria's mother was using Maria's money for herself (which wasn't true), and so Social Security took Maria's money away from her mother, Mary, all because Lynn reported this lie, and as Maria's mother had no idea and spoke Spanish, she didn't know Lynn reported them. Lynn is a very devious, dangerous, conniving person and didn't care whom she hurt.

Since Becky was also receiving a Social Security check, Lynn told her son Robert to proceed to the Social Security office the day after they arrived and change the payee's name from Becky's mother's name to his, but to their surprise, Sheila knew what was going to happen and put a stop on the check before it ever happened again (as he tried this before and succeeded). Sheila didn't know they were fighting for this until she went into court and found out they were receiving her checks. This is not the first time they tried to get Becky's check, as it's happened in the past. Can you imagine that they consider her an adult and will do anything she says knowing her mother was the payee but listens to this young man, who was twenty-seven at the time, was a thief, and had proceeded to change the payee's name? Robert's father, Larry, was also learning disabled, a thief, vicious, and violent like his son. Robert's mother, Lynn, was the brain of this family, who always wanted a girl and who is very insecure about herself. The family all went for counsel but never finished, and so the problems still exist. Lynn wanted Becky's baby, and without Becky having counsel or the permission of either of Becky's parents and she wasn't married, Lynn proceeded to adopt Becky's baby immediately and had Becky sign the papers.

Lynn decided to take Becky instead of to the airport; she took her to a doctor to find out if it's true that Becky was pregnant, as though this were her daughter. Lynn found out that Becky was five months pregnant in January when she arrived and knew the baby belonged to Robert. Becky never said anything to Sheila, so she thought she had just gained weight, and as Becky is a little heavy, it wasn't unusual. Sheila called the doctor she took Becky to in November and asked them if they have it in her records that she was pregnant, and they said no and swore that Becky was not pregnant, as they didn't have a clue that she was already three months pregnant back in November when she was there.

Can you imagine doctors not knowing whether you are pregnant or not? Sheila hit the roof, but because she didn't have Becky, there was nothing she could do. The last time Robert had sex with Becky was in August, and Lynn told Robert not to use protection. Becky was used as Lynn's surrogate mother. Lynn also found out it was a girl and this is just what she always wanted.

Lynn knew neither of them was capable of raising a child. Instead of calling Sheila, they called Becky's father to cover themselves legally as he was family, and they also thought they would get financial support from Lenny (Becky's father). Lenny never called Sheila but instead called the doctor and lied to him by telling this doctor that he is a doctor. Lenny was never a father to Becky or Becky's brother and didn't know her well as he didn't have custody of either of his children. He never paid any child support or lived near them (or knew that Becky was having stomach seizures), and he didn't know any of her problems. They lied to Becky's father as he asked them why they didn't call Sheila, and they said that Sheila didn't want any part of this baby and, of course, never told him that Sheila wanted her daughter back home and that they were to send her back as she had a round-trip ticket and had no right to take her to Crooksville. They were trying to use him for their needs, but he didn't fall for all their bullshit. What upset Sheila was that Lenny never called her to tell her what was going on. Instead, Sheila found out through Becky because Robert left his cell phone home when she came home from the hospital, Becky found it and decided to call Sheila and asked, "Why didn't you come to the hospital?" Sheila replied, "I didn't know you were there."

The problem with this is that a senator came along and initiated a law that says that you cannot get a person's medical report without that person signing a release form, and that includes a mentally challenged person. If a person is incapable of making decisions as Becky is, then the only way to get a report from a doctor is having guardianship or having that person sign for the reports, and being the mother of this person doesn't mean a thing. Once again, a complete stranger having this person in their possession can get all the reports so long as they have that person say yes. Before this law became effective, Becky's father, who bought his license in Florida to do chiropractic, got caught with drugs and was put on probation for drug-conspiracy charges and, of course, lost his license. He called the doctor who delivered Becky's baby and told him that he was a doctor and told the doctor to do a C-section on Becky, which the doctor did. When Lenny and his wife appeared at the hospital, he never called Sheila. Lenny and his wife were mad at Sheila because she kept trying for years to get child-support money and just never succeeded in getting it as he put all his assets in other people's names, plus he thought he knew Becky when he didn't. When he heard that Lynn adopted Becky's baby, he was fuming. He had a big fight with Lynn and Larry, and since Lenny would not help them financially, they cut all ties with him.

They told Becky her father was a "jerk" and made sure she would not call him either. After all the damages that were done, Sheila called him because she hadn't heard from him and thought she should talk to him.

When Sheila did call, it was then that Lenny admitted and agreed with Sheila that Becky was brainwashed and put into a cultic situation. Becky's father was very angry at the Clowns and told Sheila he couldn't make the trip to testify in court as he was dying of cancer and didn't have much time. Yet at Christmas, he made a trip to New York City and then to Florida for a vacation, and even while he was on morphine, he went golfing. He is just a liar and really doesn't care whom he hurts, and that probably is the one thing Sheila agrees with the Clowns: that he is a "jerk." But she never instilled hate into either of her kids or told them how she felt about him. In a conversation, Sheila asked him if he would go to an attorney and get a deposition done where he lived, and he said he would. Of course, he didn't, and it just meant that Sheila was fighting by herself to get Becky. Lenny is a complete waste, and so is his wife, who is on Prozac, not too bright, vicious, and was only out for themselves.

When Becky was giving birth or prior to her giving birth, Sheila was wondering what they told the doctor and what they said about the mother and if the doctor was curious to know what happened to the mother. Sheila finally got the name of the doctor and spoke to him. He was very gentle and soft-spoken and told Sheila they did say something about her but couldn't remember.

He mentioned that he spoke to Lenny on the phone and that he told him he was a doctor. After the conversation with Sheila, he felt very bad. She could hear it in his voice. The only other thing he said was that Robert was in a car accident, which didn't surprise Sheila as he has had many accidents already.

Lynn proceeded to have all the phones disconnected and wrote a letter to Sheila, saying, "I will now be Becky's mother and you will never see your daughter or speak to her again, so don't bother calling or writing to her as it will be returned, she no longer wants any part of you and she will now call me Mom." Sheila tried to get in touch with Becky, but it was impossible as they used themselves as human shields. The last time Sheila spoke to Becky, she told her that she was going to send a package out to her and to look for it. Well, needless to say, they received the package and wrote the word "refused" and sent it back to Sheila unopened.

After the baby girl was born (Sheila's granddaughter), Lynn then proceeded to immediately adopt this baby as she always wanted a girl and never told Becky's father or Sheila that she was going to do this. She kept in touch with Lenny so that Lynn could get as much money as she could out of him until she adopted the baby and cut all connections with him because she knew that when both parents found out, they would be very upset. Because Becky is considered an adult, there was nothing that either of them could do about this. Lynn knew this. Lynn then proceeded to get Becky married to Robert. Lynn knew Sheila and Lenny would also be very upset over this as Sheila already had it annulled once before. She covered herself as this was all planned, knowing that Sheila didn't have a leg to stand on since she never had guardianship. Lynn knew what she had done was wrong. Lynn didn't know while she was busy adopting the baby and getting Becky married that Sheila was trying to go for guardianship. Lynn thought she was now safe since Robert was now Becky's husband. What Lynn didn't know is that a good mother will never let her children down, and she will fight for what is right no matter what the cost is. The question is, will Sheila's attorney be able to convince the courts that Lynn stole her daughter and put her into a cultic situation and that Becky has been brainwashed? He now has to convince the courts that Lynn told Becky to tell everyone that "she wants Lynn to be her guardian," not even knowing what this means. Lynn knew that Robert could never be guardian as he is manic-depressive and bipolar and has police records, including a restraining order. Larry, Robert's father, is also mentally challenged, as is Larry's mother, who is retarded and lives in New York. Lynn never had a good relationship with her mother either. Neither Robert nor Larry could pass for being Becky's guardian.

One day, when Sheila went out to their house to see if she could get to Becky, Larry was home. Larry told Sheila "that it would be over his dead body before she ever saw her daughter again." Lynn has more of a chance of becoming guardian as compared to Robert and Larry unless proven insane and not normal herself. Lynn also realized that in order to protect all that she has done, she had better try to fight Sheila from getting guardianship. Sheila was a special education teacher and owned a couple of businesses and was an excellent mother as well as an excellent daughter. Sheila gave up her life for her children and will fight tooth and nail to protect her children.

In the state of Florida, there is no "grandparent's law," and so Becky's grandmother (Selma), who has since died, would never see her grandchild, Becky, again. In other states, they have a grandparent's law, and the one that has the most grandparents is in the state of Florida. And would you believe they took that law out of Florida? Where are those fighting grandparents who should be changing this law so this doesn't happen to anyone else?

In the state of Florida, a panel of doctors is appointed by the courts to interview and test this person to see if this person is competent. There was a panel of three people; each one saw Becky on separate days. The first person spoke to Lynn and to Becky and voiced an opinion on the report that said, "I feel that Becky's mother would be detrimental to Becky." This person did not have the right to make any comments as he never spoke to Sheila or met her, so why was he allowed to make this comment? Sheila came to the conclusion as her attorney did that two of the panelists spoke to Lynn and went according to whatever they heard from Lynn. Needless to say, they put this down on their report and have since sent copies to the other attorneys and to the judge. The third panelist mentioned that Becky wanted to go outside and talk and that she needed socialization and was confused between Sheila and Lynn. Now depositions are necessary to prove to the judge that these reports were not valid as the opinions were from the person who has brainwashed her.

In Becky's case, she has been proven incompetent, and so that part is good. They should not be allowed to make any comments, but they should just test her to see if she is incompetent. They did say Becky was incompetent, but also added comments about whatever they heard from Lynn, like Becky can travel and make decisions, which is not true. People like these should never be appointed as they can be detrimental themselves and cause so many unnecessary problems, especially since they have never met

Sheila or spoken to her, so how can they make any statements about her?

Our lives just don't always smell as pretty as a "Rose"

CHAPTER III

❖

Sheila went through the entire town that Becky was living in and spoke to every attorney and pleaded with them to please help her get guardianship, which normally would cost $2,000. But because Lynn had gotten Becky pregnant and adopted the baby and had Becky married to what we would consider a "normal" son, the guardianship will now cost $10,000 or more for this mess to be unraveled. The attorneys thought Sheila had a case but felt it was a big case, and if Becky goes into court and says she wants to be with Lynn, Sheila could lose.

Of course, these attorneys she tried to get never attempted to go any further than to write a letter stating she has a case, but they couldn't take it without explaining why they couldn't. All they had to do is find out if Becky was incompetent or competent and if she could make decisions, but they just weren't willing to fight and instead told Sheila she should look for another attorney. Then of course, you have those attorneys who would tell her to put $20,000 on their desk and they would take the case and still have doubts about winning. The question is, would you have your "normal" son marry someone who is mentally challenged and has nothing in common with your son? True, he is bipolar, manic-depressive, and is not receiving any help for him. Living with a family as dysfunctional as this certainly doesn't help any of them in any way. Lynn raised her two boys telling them what to do, how to do it, and when to do it, like puppets, and Lynn and Jerry would pull all the strings.

The background of a person is just so important to know before you consider any kind of marriage or relationship. If you come from a family of love, affection, devotion, and loyalty, then these are some of the most important things you can offer a person besides communication in a relationship. Unfortunately, neither Robert nor his brother, Lynn, or Larry comes from this kind of background.

Sheila went to one of the best attorneys two years prior in this little town called Crooksville for the first time, and he proceeded to draw up all the guardianship papers and was ready to serve Becky but needed Sheila to sign them first. Becky was not married at this time, nor was she pregnant. Sheila drove five hours to Crooksville and, on the way, called her ex-husband, Lenny, and his wife, Paula, to tell them what she was going to do, not knowing that they were going to call Lynn and Larry and warned them of what Sheila had in mind as they wanted to hurt Sheila.

Since Lenny was operated on for cancer and Paula was on Prozac, neither of them was really very happy. Lenny, Becky's father, wasn't too strong and didn't care what Paula did. Paula, who wasn't very normal, thought they should get even with Sheila for trying to get child support (that she was entitled to and that Sheila never got) by using Becky as their pawn to get even with Sheila, who was only trying to do the right thing for her daughter. The first time, before Becky became pregnant and Sheila was trying to get guardianship,

Lenny and Paula called Lynn and arranged to fly Robert and Becky to Lenny's (Sheila's ex-husband) house in Las Vegas so the attorney couldn't serve Becky. You see, in order to get guardianship, the person must live in that state in order to be served. If that person cannot be served, then you can't get guardianship.

When they got Becky in Las Vegas, they also got them married (the first time they got her married in Florida until Sheila got her back and had it annulled when she got back home. This is now the second time they remarried her which was in Vegas). Lenny & Paula invited Lynn and Larry, and would not tell Sheila what was going on, or let Becky speak to her. This is when all this nightmare started, and it wasn't until Lenny and Paula really got to know Robert did Lenny and Paula realize that Sheila and her mother were right about them, and eventually threw Robert out. But Robert convinced Becky to leave with him once again as Lenny & Paula thought she was going to continue to stay, but she didn't and left with Robert instead. She really didn't like Paula or really want to be with Lenny as her heart was really with Sheila.

What caused all this is that Robert stole Lenny's key to his boat and took it out and smashed it when he went to park it, lied to them, stole checks from Lenny, and just his bad attitude. Lenny and Paula did call Sheila after three months to tell Sheila that they were sorry for what they had done, but it was once again too late as the damage was done and had to be undone.

Sheila was disgusted as they really hurt Becky. Becky did finally call Sheila and did eventually go home, and so Sheila now had to get the marriage annulled. The judge in

Fort Lauderdale, Florida (where the annulment had to take place) told both the attorney and Sheila that she should go for guardianship, but it was at this time that Sheila took Becky and moved out of the state to Georgia, and she would now have to look for another attorney where they were living. Of course that meant more monies for Sheila and that was a problem that had to be figured out.

Because Sheila took Becky out of the state and bought a new home to be closer to her mother (Becky's grandmother), she hadn't looked into getting an attorney. Sheila and Becky were there for a month when Becky called Robert (who lived in Crooksville, Florida) and never told Sheila he was on his way to Georgia and told her would he be at the house in one hour. She also didn't tell Sheila that Robert told her to take her dog, Pebbles, a miniature pinscher, and meet him on the corner, which she did without Sheila knowing she left the house. It was important to play this cool so Becky didn't run off with Robert, and instead, Sheila acted very nice and returned back to the house. When Becky and the dog came back, she told Sheila she was going back with Robert to get his things as he planned on moving in and promised to come back. Sheila was very upset and should have called the police but thought that at least she could show Becky he wasn't very nice.

Becky being mentally young and not thinking as an adult as most youngsters was boy crazy and wasn't in love as she didn't understand what the meaning of a relationship is. Sheila who hoped she would give him up on her own was important in order for this to really work. And of course, with a little help as she was not realizing or recognizing his problems Sheila took a chance with hopes she would see the light of day and she would return, which they did. Becky, her grandmother, and Sheila went back to their other house in Florida when Becky finally got back home to Georgia and immediately left as they wanted to settle this annulment, as it was after they finally got the annulment and went back to Georgia that Sheila told Robert to move. Sheila was very upset and thought that this time it was finally over, but it wasn't.

Before Robert moved is when he got Sheila pregnant and this is when Sheila needed to get an attorney but had no idea. It was 3 months later when Becky took a trip back to Florida to see her friend and her family (who were going to watch Becky and didn't) and once again ended up with Robert who travelled 5 hours down to Ft. Lauderdale from Crooksville, Florida and met up with Becky again and this time coerced her to go back home with him that Sheila went to see this attorney and traveled hours to where he was and told him the whole story and gave him her papers and two thousand dollars to get everything started. Months would go by, and nothing was ever done. Becky had the baby and then Lynn got her remarried. This attorney lied to Sheila and told her that she was served and was waiting for the report. But nothing was ever done. The papers never left his office, and months went by.

Sheila would call him and leave messages, but there was still no response. She begged this attorney to please get started, and of course, he just gave one excuse after the other until, finally, Sheila called the Bar Association, and he returned all her money. After going back to the original attorney and having him decline her, she went still to a third attorney, who told Sheila it would cost a lot of money and that he didn't think she would win and that she ought to give up and not put good money into bad. Another attorney told Sheila that the paperwork she had was old.

Well, of course the papers were old, but then, so was Becky. Most of the attorneys would ask Sheila to send those papers of the case. Most of the attorneys gave Sheila hopes and dreams that finally this was going to be taken care of, and then with each one of her dreams was shot down by them, sending back all the papers and a letter saying she had a case but they couldn't take it. Sheila didn't give up but was exhausted mentally and needed time to breathe in between before she would continue to look again for the right attorney. Finally, after Sheila exhausted all the attorneys in this town, she went out of town again. Sheila thought she finally met the right attorney and got Becky into court. This attorney, Mr. Witchell, told Sheila he doesn't know how this is going to go but that he had a friend that had a child who is mentally challenged, and so he was very familiar with mentally challenged people and would take the case. Mr. Witchell had Becky served and had the panel of people check Becky. Then Mr. Witchell and Sheila went to court, which was a lot more than any of the other attorneys accomplished. She is so discussed and so mentally bruised that it is just so hard to be excited as she is afraid of another letdown. It's like riding a roller coaster where you never see the end or the "light at the end of the tunnel". It's so hard to relax and let the attorney who is getting paid do all the thinking for her. I guess she is afraid of another mistake and going backward again. It's scary when you have to try to convince the judge, the only person who has her life in his hands. With all the proofs, the documents, the pictures, and all the love a mother could give, the question remains, will the judge award this person the guardianship, or will he give it to the other person, Lynn, who decided to fight Sheila?

In between attorneys, Sheila even contacted Governor Jeb Bush and Zell Miller and wrote to the *Montel Williams Show,* *The Oprah Winfrey Show,* and *Good Morning America* as she felt that with Elizabeth Smart a fourteen year old, who was stolen from her home and brainwashed in eight months and got the AMBER Law put into effect immediately, which should have included those that are mentally challenged. Senator Zell Miller received five letters explaining how Sheila went to attorneys and investigators and could not get help, but as with most of our representatives, Senator Miller wrote back, saying "he was sorry and that I should get an Attorney." Sheila realized he did not read her letters as Senator Miller was told she went to at least seven attorneys and couldn't get help and it would cost a lot of money and there is no legal aid for this kind of case or agencies and if he could possibly help.

Gov. Jeb Bush doesn't read his mail and has others do it for him. His aides could do nothing but tell Sheila to e-mail him and that he would get back to her. His aide did e-mail and told her there are *no* agencies that could help.

Unfortunately time just doesn't stand still and we need to move on and keep alert and do the right thing and be the winner.

CHAPTER IV

❖

The last time, before Becky left to visit her girlfriend in Florida, she wrote a couple of letters saying how happy she was back to live home and loved her room. She wrote letters telling Sheila how much she loved her. Becky was raised with love, affection, devotion, and communication. Becky went to private schools, speech therapists, learned to swim at three years old, and even went to a dude ranch and went horseback riding, roller skating, dancing, and bowling. Becky used to go away with her grandparents to a summer home on a lake in Maine, so she would go fishing on her grandfather's boat and tried to water-ski as everyone tried to teach her, but she was too afraid and would let go of the rope. Never would they make her feel inadequate or make her feel ashamed as the Clowns are doing to her today by calling her retarded and telling her to shut up. Her grandparents, who the kids called, Granny and Papa, would take Becky and her brother to auctions, movies and clambakes, and even fishing. They would go on picnics and travel around to see different things, such as the "Old Man in the Mountain" in New Hampshire. There was no reason Becky would be unhappy except if she were brainwashed. When both Sheila's children would return home after the summer, they would get all new clothes for school and for vacations. Sheila would take them to Busch

Gardens or Disney World or shows and even concerts, but more recently, Sheila would take Granny and the two children to Tennessee or through parts of Georgia. This time around, Lynn and Robert took all her pictures of her past away from her, all her phone numbers, and whatever jewelry Sheila gave her that Robert didn't steal and sell. Becky was very lucky as she really had everything.

The funny thing is that Becky never liked Robert, and tried very hard to get away from him. Becky once told some friends that she didn't want to be with him and even had them beat him up and called the police on him for being abusive to her. Robert and his family lived in New Jersey before they lived in Florida, and Robert had dated another girl that was also disabled and whose mother got a restraining order against him as Robert was also on drugs at this time. Sheila didn't know at the beginning how bad Robert was, and she knew Becky had liked another boy, who was from Mexico, and wanted to be with him. Sheila realized this boy didn't speak English well and thought that Becky was physically normal. He didn't know she was mentally challenged, because of the language barrier. When Sheila saw he was talking about marriage, Sheila became concerned about this relationship and felt this relationship needed to be broken up since it wasn't fair to this young man as he was a "normal" young man who had no clue. Sheila found out later that he was deported to Mexico, and so that explained why he also wanted to marry Becky. Not knowing Robert, Sheila thought maybe she should push Becky toward him as he had a family and lived in the United States and seemed nice but found out they weren't very nice and needed to get Becky away from them.

Sheila couldn't afford guardianship, so it had to wait until she could afford it, besides the fact that Becky moved out of the state of Georgia Sheila would have to start all over again looking for an attorney in Florida where Becky was living as a temporary until she got back with Becky to Georgia. Sheila also had other things that needed to be done for the future of her family, not knowing what was going to happen, she put the guardianship on the back burner in Georgia. When Larry, Lynn and Robert decided to keep Becky the war began and so it was at this time that Sheila got Mr. Witchell who was an Attorney in Florida that was near Becky and started proceedings.

Sheila now has to go into court in Crooksville, Florida to fight not only for her to be guardian but also thought she had to prove why Robert shouldn't be guardian, until she got into court, not knowing that she was going to be fighting Lynn (Robert's mother). Then Mr. Witchell the Attorney, called Sheila to confirm that Lynn, not Robert, is going to fight for guardianship. Lynn knows that Robert is not qualified and realizes that if Sheila wins and becomes guardian, then she would reverse the adoption of the baby, have the marriage annulled once again, and then have Becky sue this family for the damages they have done to her and Sheila. Becky will need a good physiologist as they have ruined Becky. Becky has been programmed by Lynn into telling people and the court-appointed attorney that she wants Lynn as her guardian, when Becky doesn't understand what the meaning of "guardian" is or what the consequences could be. The court-appointed attorney for Becky thought for some reason that he could represent Lynn as his client as well as Becky, but it was a conflict of interest, and so after, he did the damage of submitting the paperwork for Lynn to the courts that she wanted to be guardian.

When Mr. Witchell told the judge it was a conflict of interest, it was thrown out of court. Mr. Witchell should have also eliminated Becky's attorney as well because he already has caused damages to Sheila and her case, but Mr. Witchell never did, and this was just the beginning of numerous mistakes Mr. Witchell made. There really is no more room for mistakes, but so many were made after this hearing. It was pathetic.

Lynn was told she had five days to call another attorney as Sheila already spoke to this attorney and it was a conflict of interest. It wasn't until after this that Sheila realized that there is no one in town that Lynn could use because Sheila had already spoken to all of them, so the judge told Lynn that if she doesn't get another attorney, it will be thrown out of court and then she couldn't go for guardianship. Sheila really felt so good about this, but instead of it getting better, it got worse. The next hearing was with a different judge and a new attorney that Lynn got through Becky's attorney, who was from another town nearby. Because Mr. Witchell didn't say anything at the next hearing, Sheila became frustrated and yelled out to the judge, "May I speak, Your Honor?" the judge looked up and said *no*, and after that, you could hear a pin drop and the judge continuing to say he doesn't see any difference in what the three panelists reported. Sheila poked Mr. Witchell in the stomach to tell him there is a difference, but instead, he just sat there and said nothing. There wasn't enough time allotted in this day of court, so it was postponed for another hearing and so everyone left. Now it was two friends (attorneys) against Sheila and Mr. Witchell since Sheila got this attorney through Becky's attorney.

This was the first time in three and a half years that Sheila saw Becky and Becky never made eye contact with Sheila. Instead, she would look up at the ceiling, but not at Sheila as she was told not to look at Sheila. Sheila walked up to Becky and told her how pretty she looked. Becky told Sheila that she was angry, very angry with her, and so Sheila asked Becky why she was so angry with her, and Becky, noticing a cat pin Sheila was wearing, told her, "Because you called me a dog or cat." Sheila just couldn't think fast enough and should have said "Becky, I haven't spoken to you in almost three and a half years, and the last time I did, if you remember, you asked me if I were going to see you, and I told you I couldn't but I was going to send you a package. If I called you anything, it would have been 'pussycat' as an affectionate word, but why would I call you a dog or cat?" Sheila was more taken aback that Becky didn't even look at her, and of course, as Lynn was right there, it wasn't comfortable. Sheila didn't let this get to her as she knew what Lynn, Larry, and Robert had done to her.

Sheila believed Becky was ready to explode and doesn't know whom to talk to and how to express her emotions; Sheila saw Lynn take Becky into another area and kept Becky away from Sheila after Mr. Witchell called Sheila, and it was because he thought Becky told her to leave her alone, which Sheila said "she never did." Later, Lynn and Becky were standing and talking to Becky's attorney when Lynn yelled out to the attorney, saying, "She's on drugs." And Sheila was sure this was referring to her, who doesn't even take her vitamins like she should. Sheila is over sixty-one years old and looks very good for her age, as most people think she is in her fifties. She dresses like a celebrity and has the jewelry to go with each outfit she wears, yet she is very simple as her hair is brown and very short and wispy with the biggest brown eyes, but this ordeal has changed her looks. Sheila is a very gentle, intelligent person who graduated from college and who became a special education teacher who has the patience of a saint. Sheila has friends that are authors, accountants, project directors building libraries for the disadvantaged children, lawyers, judges, and other professionals whom she has known from thirty years to forty years of her life. After much thought of why Lynn took Becky in the other room away from everyone, which was to prep Becky and tell her, "If your mother tries to talk to you, you are to turn your back on her" which was just another way of brain washing Becky by turning her against her Mother and instilling bad thoughts into Becky and scaring her and using Blackmail by also adding she would never see her child again if she doesn't listen and do as she was told.

Sheila knew that after the three and a half years, Lynn now became her authority figure; the one Becky now has no choice but to listen to, the person who knows how to push her buttons and treat her like a puppet and pull her strings. Sheila was sick to her stomach and just didn't know what to do without getting into trouble. Sheila calmed herself down and tried to go on without thinking of the worst and kept telling herself that Mr. Witchell will get her daughter back and it will be done legally.

Life is so short and so is this Magnolia that seems so pretty and bright.
Every moment counts so make each one just as important as the next.

CHAPTER V

Lynn is a 250-pound woman who is fifty-eight, who looks like she is in her sixties, with gray hair that looks like she never brushed it, and dresses as though she just went through the Goodwill garbage can to get an outfit together. Lynn works for the city of Crooksville as someone who orders equipment for the city. She is a terrible liar as she has lied not only to Becky, but also to her boss, to her children, to her family, and to strange people she meets. Lynn has no friends or families that she socializes with and lets her family think she can do no wrong. At one time, she got Robert a job in her office to clean up the place at night. He sure did clean it up; he took a radio and anything else he could find. The next day, Lynn's boss approached Lynn about it, and so Lynn went home and took the things back and told her boss she found it in another room but didn't know why and, of course, never punished Robert as though it was okay.

Lynn called up work one day before all this and told her boss she was sick, which was a total lie as she went out of state to visit her sister. Instead, Lynn called Sheila because Sheila told the truth to her boss, but Lynn cried and begged her to please call her boss back and tell her that she made a mistake and it wasn't true that she went out of town, because she thought she was going to be fired. Sheila felt she had to or she wouldn't get Becky back, being that this was another time she tried to keep her, so she now had Sheila lie to her boss. During the conversation, her boss told Sheila she had a child that was also mentally challenged and understood, and then Sheila had to tell her boss she lied when she really didn't. Sheila felt bad that she called her boss back, but there was nothing she could do about it.

There were two times that these people tried to get Sheila's daughter, and it was the second time—the last, which is now—that they really succeeded in keeping Becky away from all of Sheila's family and friends. Becky was coerced each time by Robert and Lynn, and now here it is—a nightmare of four years that is finally coming to an end. Sheila moved out of the state and got Becky away with hopes of some relief from all this. One of the attorneys said to Sheila, "What would you do if Becky runs away?" Sheila looked at the attorney, and all she could do was roll her eyes as if to say Becky is not capable. After all this, she would make sure she got a restraining order to keep the Clowns away and let Becky know that she cannot call them for any reason. But it just never happened. Becky, as a stupid teenager, went against her mother's wishes and called Robert. But Becky doesn't act defiantly, and 99 percent of the time, she will listen, especially if that person is a strong person or pushes the right buttons. Can you imagine someone coming along and stealing your child and getting away with it? It's like you are drowning and you don't have any help and you try to get out but can't because every time you try, another wave comes on top of you and weighs you down.

June 16, 2004

Here it is—one week after the first round at the courthouse, and all that Sheila can think of is how she handled her first meeting with Becky. Sheila's wheels have been spinning, and she was thinking what she would have done differently with Becky when she first saw her. Sheila felt so uncomfortable and really didn't know how Becky would react to Sheila if she "said 'Come on and give me a hug'" as she would have done in the past. I think she was afraid of a bad reaction with all the people around and that it wouldn't have looked good, and even though she ignored Lynn, she felt the tension. The fact that Lynn took Becky in another area to talk to her and keep her from her mother didn't look good either. Sheila was so afraid that there would be a problem especially when Mr. Witchell went over a couple of times to get Sheila away and just didn't understand why. Sheila really was trying to decide if she should hug Becky, but she felt Becky acted like a stranger and Sheila just didn't know her anymore, nor did she know how to act. Sheila's heart sank in her stomach, and so she did nothing as sometimes doing nothing is better than doing the wrong thing. Sheila just felt so sad and knew Becky had been programmed, and Becky just didn't respond as she would have. Yes, Sheila was angry too, and it had a lot to do with all the coldness and hatred in the room that Lynn instilled in Becky. The fact that Becky wouldn't even make eye contact with Sheila was very disturbing to her, and it didn't help. The more Sheila thinks, the worse it is because she has no one to discuss this with to get it out of her system in order for her to go on with the strength she really needs.

All Sheila can think of is how she gave up all her dreams and expectations because of how a family thinks they can steal someone else's child/adult. Sheila is a single parent and took on the jobs of a mother, father, teacher, butler, maid, and chauffeur. She worked two and three jobs to make her children happy. She looks back at these last few years, and all she can think of is the waste of time, energy, and thousands of dollars that could have gone to better places if only she went for guardianship. The hate that has been instilled in Becky and the hate that Sheila has also developed from all this are beyond your wildest dreams. Yes, she is also very disappointed in Becky, but then she must keep telling herself that she is being brainwashed and it could happen to even a "normal" person, so why should Becky be any different? Working two and three jobs to support both of Sheila's children is not as hard as this.

No parent should have to pay one penny to become guardian, and no parent must be made to feel that all the work they have done was fruitless.

A parent, as a result, gets all the pain and anguish and very little happiness, unlike the normal child you raise and hope for. You force yourself to smile and laugh and just pray for the best, whereas a stranger is looking for the check or for their own satisfaction (control) and really doesn't care what happens to that child. No one in this world could love this young adult more than the real/adopted parent can. It wasn't the stranger who gave up their life; it was the parent that said "I don't think I can go out and leave my child alone and include them in whatever I do." Most strangers will have a motive; this word is not in a parent's vocabulary. The fact that

Becky said she was very angry with Sheila and did not know why and did not look at her shows the beginning of many problems that had occurred with Becky. I am sure Becky was told not to look at her mother as she could see Robert doing this and telling Becky to do this. Sheila was lucky that she did speak to every attorney in this town so it would make it very hard for Lynn to find one in this town. But she did not do this deliberately or with any motives; it just happened. If anyone steals your child, you jump on it, and don't ever give up letting all your work go down the drain. If anything, a parent should be awarded for the great job they have done. They should get a medal for giving up their life to make someone else's life happier.

I thought "all good things come to an end", but it is not true,
there are still many good things that go on with hopes,
dreams and prays and a good fight.

CHAPTER VI

Becky's grandmother, whom she loved, died after she left, and Lynn wouldn't return Becky even after knowing that her grandmother had a heart attack. Becky's grandmother (Granny as they called her) was 5'2" with wispy short gray hair. She was intelligent, witty, and charming and was in a nursing home when Sheila went to see her. She said, "Sheila, I think Becky was here." It was so sad to know that she would never see her granddaughter again. Sheila, in a very gentle voice, said "Mom, Becky is in Florida" just to remind her. Granny said "Oh" and made a face of just disgust. Her Mother was eighty-five on May 20, 2001, and looked as though she were seventy-five. She died at 1:00 a.m. on May 21, 2001. Becky's daughter, Sheila's granddaughter, was born on May 22, 2001, the day after Granny died. In Sheila's religion, when a person dies, you name the new baby after that person so their soul rests in peace. Lynn told Sheila in a letter that she won't name the baby after anyone in the family, and she didn't.

Lenny, who was in remission from cancer, now has it back again. But this time, there isn't anything more that can be done for him, so it's just a matter of time before he dies. When Sheila saw Becky, she told her that her father was dying, but Becky still didn't make any eye contact and didn't express any feelings. Sheila does believe Becky is angry but just doesn't understand why. Lynn has told her things about her family, and now she has no one to ask and has to learn to accept whatever they have told her. One of the doctors who saw Becky said she had a speech impediment, and at first, Sheila said it was a language-development problem. When she spoke to Becky, Becky told Sheila that she was very angry with Sheila and said that one of the reasons is because she called her a dog or a cat. Sheila was concerned about her speech. Sheila is wondering if she now has a speech impediment, and if she does, Sheila thinks it may be caused by this whole situation that is caused by the Clowns. Sheila said that when she meets Becky again, she will, this time, see if she can give her a hug. She thought about this as well since it didn't happen when she saw Becky the first time. Sheila was just being careful that she didn't fall into a trap, like Lynn or Robert telling her, "Don't let your mother hug you and don't look at her," which would again make herself look like the bad guy. Going back in the past when Robert and Becky went to Vegas, they returned and got a restraining order against Sheila.

Robert and Lynn wrote the story and insisted that Becky sign it, not knowing what they wrote nor having any understanding of it. In any event, Becky had no idea what all this would cause. When Robert and Becky and Sheila went to court, the judge threw out the restraining order as he realized Sheila was okay and never did anything to hurt Becky.

The last time she spoke to Becky on the phone, Becky asked Sheila if she were going to see her, and Sheila knew that Robert was up to no good as he was right there with her, and if she came around, they would lock her up for trespassing or harassment. So she told Becky she couldn't and that she loved her and was going to send her a package. Sheila was very paranoid that if she went to hug Becky, there could have been a problem, so because of her feelings, she backed off. The next time they see each other; Sheila will hug Becky and let her know how sorry she is that Becky is so angry. It won't be necessarily in this order as she has to think about getting Becky off guard from what Lynn is telling her to do.

Maybe they will not remind Becky about hugging her mother as they might have already done the first time and to look at this as the expression goes, "Forewarned is forearmed," so that the next time, it will be unexpected from the first. The next time is going to be the most important one, with hopes it will be when Sheila gets good news from the hearing in October that Sheila's attorney will be allowed to do depositions, and of course, these will be successful. Sheila has been put through the wringer with the Clowns and feels for Becky and knows the hurt Becky has been going through, so Sheila has all those feelings in her that Becky should be having, but feels she has been made into a puppet. I guess she feels that all the fears and the anxiety and hopes and dreams are just so exhausting and that the humiliation of all this is just beyond belief. The prayers are so numerous among friends and family and complete strangers, with hopes the courts will see all this and be on her side. Sheila just prays that Becky will wake up and realize that Sheila and her family are fighting because they have so much love for Becky and feels the Clowns are trying to destroy her and all those that really love her as they have done with each other.

Sheila said the waiting is the most horrific feeling, the unexpected and the not knowing if you are going to win or not and what will you do if you don't win. "I don't know how the other side feels," she said, but only they know, and they will have to live with what they have done to a family whether they win or not. Sheila said her feeling is like the clock stopped and everyone around is just so still that you can hear a pin drop. Sheila says it is so hard to even breathe because even though it has gotten so close, it just seems so far. Her chest is so heavy and outweighs everything, and she wishes she would feel better about everything, and that is because she has so many concerns to think about and wishes there was someone she could talk to who knew the answers. No one can imagine what a parent goes through when their child is alive and you can't get to see them or speak to them or write to them. When you don't have communication and there is a complete breakdown, it's as though the person has died. You try to put them out of your mind, yet as when someone dies, still throughout the years, little things come up to remind you of your loved one. And when you realize they are alive, you hope that the other person still loves you and really doesn't want to give you up. You hope that they still have some memories of the past and that it will help strengthen them with each meeting and you pray for that little thread of a feeling that is still alive to pop out and say something, hopefully, like "I love you." Sheila hopes Becky has a little piece of that thread left in her so Sheila can grab it, and of course, that is if she has the opportunity, which I do believe no one can stop at this time.

This flower will die as another will grow and as they say,
"when one door closes another will open". It is so important to
continue what you started and never give up and open those doors.

CHAPTER VII

❖

How can you fight something when you don't know what you are up against? You can only fight when you know what it is and when you don't know the ultimate surprise of what it could be; it is saddening when you are not prepared. It's important to do your homework and make sure it's correct. The Clowns stole not only Sheila's daughter but also her daughter's heart, from what Sheila can see.

Sheila is betting on the love that Becky has for her and the saying "Blood is thicker than water." Sheila doesn't know the amount of damage they have done to Becky and is really so concerned.

October 29

Sheila went to the next hearing, and Mr. Witchell said "nothing" except when the judge mentioned the panelist. He then said he would like to do their depositions, but the judge said he didn't think this was necessary but that if he wanted to have them do an addendum to the original reports, he could do this. Before each hearing, Lynn would get Becky all mad again so she could react to the situation. People like Becky can't remember what happened yesterday, so they don't hold a grudge. Sheila was very upset with her attorney because he did not represent her as he should have. She couldn't believe all those plans and expectations of what was going to be were totally down the drain like everything else. He said "nothing." Absolutely nothing! Sheila made her long trip back home in a complete daze. The third hearing was supposed to be the final hearing, and still, her attorney never spoke up, and so the judge heard nothing once again! He didn't even know that Sheila was a special education teacher and had Becky for thirty years, and he didn't know all the dirty things Lynn did. At the final hearing, the judge bent over and said to Mr. Witchell, "I don't think it's necessary for Sheila to speak." And all Mr. Witchell did was nod his head as though he felt it wouldn't have made a difference.

Sheila didn't hear his response, and the judge awarded Lynn with a partial guardianship. When they all left the judge's chambers, Sheila called, "Becky," when Lynn turned around and said, "Leave us alone." Sheila called Becky again but, this time, in a very low voice. Becky said, "Leave me alone." Sheila was really upset and told Mr. Witchell to appeal this. Mr. Witchell asked for more money, but Sheila didn't have it and had no intentions of giving more to Mr. Witchell as she felt he owed her this for not representing her properly, and it seemed to her that the attorney was now trying to milk her as he still had $2,000 he was supposed to use for depositions that he never did. When Mr. Witchell tried to get more money out of Sheila, she told Mr. Witchell he owes her money and that he is to ask for a rehearing. Mr. Witchell submitted the paperwork, but when Sheila saw this, she told Mr. Witchell he needed to add more to explain to the judge why, and so he said he would write an addendum to it. The judge approved a rehearing that was set to be right after Christmas. Lynn's attorney wrote to the judge, telling him that he couldn't make this date and to see if he could make it for a different date, which was set for the second of February.

This time, Sheila went to the courthouse with the guy named Mike, whom she has been with on and off and who helped raise her children for thirty-one years. Mike is a 6'1" sixty-one-year-old man with gray hair, brown eyes, mustache, and glasses and is slim and very distinguished looking.

Sheila was so upset, being that Mike made this trip to give Sheila moral support and to see Becky with hopes they could do this together when they arrived in the courthouse Mr. Witchell never told Sheila he received a letter saying that Becky and Lynn did not have to be there and realized that this was going to be a total waste of time as Mike thought he would see Becky. The three attorneys met inside the courtroom, including Mike and Sheila and then the judge. Sheila thought this time would be her opportunity to speak. This was the first time Mr. Witchell finally mentioned to the judge that Sheila was a special education teacher, and Sheila yelled out she had Becky for thirty years.

The judge, once again, would not hear anything today as he said as he bent his head down, "I might have made a mistake, but I am not going to change my order, but you can appeal." Lynn's attorney told Mr. Witchell that he has said nothing except that Becky was "mind-manipulated" and he wasn't going to let him add anything else. He told Mr. Witchell what he could have done but the could-haves are just too late. Sheila was sick and realized she just lost her daughter and never got to speak to her or hug her.

Sheila will not give up unless there are no other options. Right now, all she can think of is how this woman is getting away with stealing her daughter and how everyone has turned their back on her because Lynn brainwashed Becky into telling everyone she wants to live in Florida. Sheila would love to live in Hawaii, but that doesn't mean it's the right thing to do. How can they make the ward have the option to say where they want to live? When Becky was allowed to call her father, she would call and complain about her situation, and now she can't even call him or her brother because they have spoken badly about them too. What Lynn and her family done to Becky to change her from a bubbly, friendly, lovable young lady to one that is just so angry with those that have done nothing but love her and teach her and have given up their lives for her? This woman even lied to Lenny and Paula about Sheila and had them against Sheila until they found out the truth and then took a 100% turn to protect Sheila instead of going against her. Lenny was dying and didn't have much time but he lived long enough to where he moved to Florida not that far from Larry & Lynn and with Becky's brother also moving not too far where Becky was it gave an opening to Becky to call her Father who in turn called her Brother since he was dying and told him to go and pick up Becky as she is ready to go home and so he did and Becky finally made it back to Sheila with the help of Becky's Father who called his son who went to get her and who called Sheila and told her he got Becky. Becky has been home for 8 years and is extremely happy and has never again contacted Robert or this family again.

This woman and her family really should have been put away as she is the one who is detrimental. I guess that is just another story.

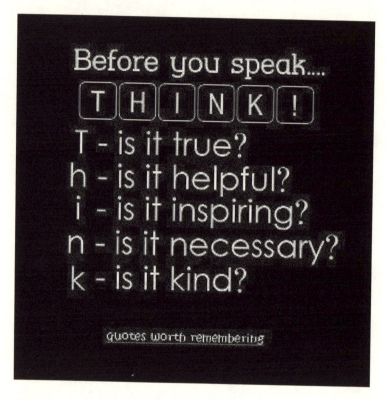

We all make mistakes but these are lessons for us to learn by and so long as we learn from our mistakes we will be good to move on, just remember, "First time shame on you, next time shame on me".

CONCLUSION

Sheila thought she lost her daughter because of the bad representation, which Mr. Witchell admitted to Sheila as he made lots of mistakes and then informed Sheila he didn't know how to do an appeal. Sheila wanted him to get help because he owed her this, but instead, he told her how one attorney would not do it and another said he would need $10,000 to $15,000 up front. Mr. Witchell told Sheila she would be wasting her money and that he didn't see it being any better than it is right now. Sheila lost the guardianship because of the lack of professionalism and because the courts refused to hear the parent's side of what had happened, as there was no communication and because of a very poor counselor. Sheila doesn't feel the courts prevailed to do justice as they refused to hear Becky's mother by not letting her speak. The ward of the court, who is Becky, has the right to say where they want to live, according to the laws of the guardianship. If they went according to the guardianship laws, which also state that they would prefer a person who is a professional and who has had special education and that the person should be a blood relative, Sheila would have qualified except the attorney never told the courts.

The panelist who said that Sheila was detrimental finally spoke to Sheila and is willing to meet with the other panelists to see if there is anything they can do. They all said that Becky can travel, and why they said this is beyond Sheila because this is not true. When Becky would travel, Sheila would buy the ticket, go to the airport, and make sure that someone is on the other side waiting for her. Mr. Witchell could have disputed this when they first submitted their reports, but he didn't.

Sheila is very, very divested and disappointed, but there is nothing else she could have done. She would like to prevent anyone else from going through what she has gone through. The courts should have heard both parties to see whom they felt would be the better guardian since the panelists are only supposed to meet with the ward and tell the courts if they feel this person is incompetent, and not give their opinions as to who is detrimental, especially since they never met or spoke to this person. The laws need to be changed and fixed to protect our young adults.

Mr. Witchell refused to continue the case with Sheila after all the damages he did in not getting rid of the court-appointed attorney at the beginning and telling the courts that this is a very unusual guardianship and explaining what had happened and giving the background of Sheila after she begged him to.

Sheila had gotten a phone call from her son Sam who asked Sheila if she were sitting down, because he just got a call from his Dad who told him that Becky wanted to come home and to please pick her up. Lenny told Sam to go and pick her up as he couldn't because of he wasn't feeling good. Apparently Becky got the courage to call because she was alone and felt she had to sneak out and both her Father and her brother were now living in Florida near Becky. Sheila was speechless and very excited and immediately packed her bag and proceeded to wait for the next call to pick her up. Sam was going to bring her over to Lenny's house as he wanted to see her before Sheila arrived.

When Sheila went to pick up Becky from Lenny in Florida he realized how wrong he was and apologized to Sheila for believing these people and for what he put everyone through and then died two days later.

Sheila then told Mr. Witchell she got Becky back and he immediately set it up for both Becky & Sheila to go back to court with Mr. Witchell (who owed this to Sheila) and really was happy for Becky and Sheila because having Becky made it so much easier and happier getting the Guardianship away from Lynn Clown and changed it to be in the state of Georgia where Becky and Sheila were going to live.

Robert and Becky were divorced once again and Robert went off with another girl whose son was mentally challenged and was also receiving a Social Security Disability check. Lynn & Larry Clown ended up with Robert and Sheila's baby as she is now 10 years old.

Becky is now living a very happy life with her Mother trying to make up for lost time and enjoying every moment together.

The moral of this story is to "get the guardianship" before your child is eighteen and don't take chances on losing your child and don't give up no matter what.

There are no footsteps in the snow, but with the,
"light at the end of the tunnel" and doing the right thing and never
giving up and doing my homework I know that this time next year
there will be lots of foot prints.

SYNOPSIS

❖

Sheila, who was a Special Education Teacher, lives outside the city of Westbrook, Maine, in a small country village. Sheila worked two and three jobs when she was raising her two children. She also became a medical assistant, a photographer, worked in restaurants, sold items for five years at the flea market, and devoted her life to her two children. She has a son who became a project director for the shows on the ships, doing all the sound and lighting effects. Sheila's daughter, Becky, who is "mentally challenged," is also physically normal and has learned to swim, dance, and bowl because of Sheila. Sheila even took sign language courses together with Becky (her daughter), thinking Becky could become a teacher's aide with the hearing-impaired. Trying to see how to change or improve the laws, Sheila made a trip to Washington, DC, and spoke to a few senators, but the timing was wrong as it was before the elections. She researched the laws and found out that there are some issues that needed to be straightened out for the sake of other children that have been put into similar situations. There are twenty thousand children who have been put into "cultic situations" or "cults." And who knows how many are mentally challenged or easily swayed young adults that have left their homes for no reason at all except to foresee new adventures, not knowing they will never have contact with their families again or realizing the consequences.

Sheila's daughter has been with her for thirty years and reads and writes according to a third and fourth grader and whose IQ is 57 and has been in special education classes. Her daughter was "coerced, brainwashed, mind-manipulated, exploited, and alienated from her family and friends." A family called the Clowns, who live in Florida in an out-of-the-way town called Crooksville, has two sick sons and has always wanted a girl. They stole Sheila's daughter by cutting all communications and not allowing her family to contact her or letting her contact them. When Lynn Clown and Lynn's son, Robert Clown, found that Becky made a few phone calls to her mother, she told her, "No more calls." And they took away all her phone numbers and then proceeded to take all the phones out of the house and just keep for themselves a couple of cell phones. They watched her 24-7 so that she could not have any communication and put her into a situation where she only had them to turn to. Becky was not the only girl they tried to steal as there were two others, but they didn't succeed as they did with Becky.

It has been three and a half years since Sheila actually spoke to her daughter, who loved her mother very much, but now the Clowns have instilled hate into her about her family and made Becky very angry with Sheila because of the things Lynn and Robert would say about her mother. The names have been changed to protect some of those involved in this story, but the story is very real. Sheila had tried very hard to get help from the police, investigators, private investigators, and attorneys but to no avail. Because Sheila is over eighteen and is considered an adult (even though she is mentally challenged), her mother never did get guardianship. The Clowns told Becky to tell everyone she did not want to see her mother, and so when the police heard she didn't want to see or speak to her mother, they could not insist because she was over eighteen. Sheila has letters written by Lynn, saying, "You are considered her ex-Mother and she is now considered your ex-daughter and now she calls me 'Mom.' You will not be allowed to see, speak or write to her." Larry Clown (Lynn's husband) told Sheila it would be over his dead body before she would ever see her daughter again.

As time went on, it got worse as they got her pregnant, adopted her baby (before she was married), and kept her from her family and friends. It wasn't until after the adoption that they got her married to the father (which was annulled once before) and to one of their sons who is manic-depressive and bipolar and would use Sheila's daughter as a sex toy and use her money. This young man is considered a "normal" boy. Sheila would think, "What would a 'normal' person have in common with someone that is 'retarded' and not able to have complete conversations with or one who can't make proper decisions?" They used her as a surrogate mother, a nanny, and as a "puppet so they can pull her strings and have learned how to push her buttons, telling her what to do, how to do it, and when to do it," as this was one of Larry's expressions.

Sheila has this inner feeling that she needs to warn the people who are in similar situations and hopes she can do justice for them by letting people know that getting "guardianship" is very important to have no matter what the cost is (although they should shop around for an attorney but not lose too much time in doing so). It is important to protect this person from those that can steal someone else's young adult since they can get away with it, but before this happens, they need to learn how to go about protecting their young adult as there are no agencies out there for young adults, which was confirmed with Gov. Jeb Bush's office in Florida and with other states.

Sheila is hoping someone will read this and help change the laws and have agencies out there that will help, but until then, parents need to nip this in the bud. Sheila can't stress this enough and just not do what she did, and that is to "put guardianship on the back burner."

Waiting, Hoping and Dreaming is not a bad thing, especially when it all works out for the best. There is nothing like being the Winner, get the prize and have that prize be just as happy as you.